THE
DIESEL
YEARS

ROBERT P. OLMSTED

Golden West Books
San Marino, California

THE DIESEL YEARS

Copyright © 1975 by Robert P. Olmsted
All Rights Reserved
Published by Golden West Books
San Marino, California 91108 U.S.A.

Library of Congress Catalog Card No. 75-17721
I.S.B.N. 0-87095-054-1

CIP

Library of Congress Cataloging in Publication Data

Olmsted, Robert P
    The Diesel years.

    1. Diesel locomotives--History--Pictorial works.
2. Locomotives--United States--History--Pictorial
works. I. Title.
TJ619.O394   385'.36'60973   75-17721
ISBN 0-87095-054-1

FRONT END PAGES — Baltimore & Ohio 1409 at Grand Central Station in Chicago in August 1965. *FRONTISPIECE* — Brand new Santa Fe FP45 100 eases into Corwith Yard, Chicago, with an eastbound freight in January 1968. This was a break-in run for the unit. *TITLE PAGE* — PA's 70 and 68 lean into a curve near Lemont, Illinois, with Santa Fe Train 24, formerly the *Grand Canyon Limited*, but now nameless in this January 1968 scene. *REAR END PAGES* — On April 18, 1962, Chicago, Burlington & Quincy E5 9915B was assigned to the westbound *Nebraska Zephyr* out of Chicago. Gleaming in the morning sun, the E5 leads two newer EMD E-units and Train 11 out of Union Station, about to begin the daylight dash to Omaha.

Golden West Books

A Division of Pacific Railroad Publications, Inc.

P.O. BOX 8136 • SAN MARINO, CALIFORNIA • 91108

4

TABLE OF CONTENTS

Rock Island's well known E6 630, in bright red and gold paint with silver side panels, heads the *Golden Rocket* excursion near Putnam, Illinois, on September 10, 1972.

FOREWORD

Many sources indicate that the first successful diesel-electric locomotive in America was built in 1924 by the General Electric Company containing an Ingersoll-Rand engine; and that diesel-electric locomotives first entered revenue service in 1925. In this case either 1974 or 1975 would be the 50th anniversary of the first diesel-electric locomotive in the United States, that is depending upon which date you consider of the greater magnitude. Just a few years ago, in 1972 to be exact, the Electro-Motive Division of General Motors celebrated the 50th anniversary of their entry into the railroad field. I believe it appropriate to present a few remarks and some photographs portraying the diesel age in the United States to this historic point in time.

In recent years railroad books concerned with the diesel-electric locomotive in America have been divided into two general groupings. First you have the photographic book depicting the changeover

years from steam motive power to that of the diesel. Many of these books show only a photograph or two of any one type of diesel locomotive. Secondly, there is an increasing crop of motive power annuals and periodicals of one sort or another along the general line of providing motive power information only. These books contain a roster type illustration (a broadside or three-quarter side view) and usually a limited number of other types of photographs that show the power in service.

In this book I have taken certain specific locomotive models from each of five of the largest builders of diesel locomotives and provided a broader range of photographs of these units in service. In some cases where a larger number of units were built, I have narrowed the coverage down to only those of a certain railroad or era, and so forth. I have also chosen models which provide a range of differences in appearance and which allow a large number of railroads to be represented.

During the 1950's, when the diesel locomotive was methodically replacing steam power, it was often heard that "all diesels look the same" and "the only difference is in the color of the exterior paint." Road power, both freight and passenger, was almost universally a cab-type unit with enclosed access to the machinery. The yard switchers from most builders came with an end cab and a low hood with outside access to the machinery in the hood. From the 1950's into the mid-1960's, however, variety became more the keynote. Hood-type road units came into favor, generally becoming more numerous than the cab units. These hood units were similar to switchers in that they had outside access to the machinery in a long hood, but they had an offset cab with a short hood on the other end. Some hood units had a high short nose, while some came with a cut-down short nose. Units from all the builders were still in service and most firms had new and somewhat different appearing models each year or so.

Today, the variety seems to be decreasing again. The older cab units (often called "covered wagons") are fast disappearing. Many of the locomotive models from some of the builders are even extinct; three of the firms have left the field; and the new locomotive models coming from the only remaining builders, Electro-Motive Division and General Electric, are changing little from year to year. At any rate, the past fifty years have brought quite an overall variety in the diesel look as I hope the following pages will illustrate.

A general history of the activities of each builder is included in the appropriate section on the following pages. A complete condensed time table of these activities by year may be found on the last page of this book.

All of the photographs in this volume are by the author unless otherwise credited; and the accuracy of the accompanying data is my responsibility. A large measure of credit and thanks should go to Donald Duke for assuming the burden of putting this book together and its eventual publication. A word of appreciation is extended to Burdell Bulgrin and to James Farrell for providing transportation and some fine times during the outings while taking a number of the photographs in this book. Richard Simak and Charles Krubl are responsible for most of the great photographic prints used in the production of half-tones. And finally a special note of thanks to my wonderful family, Carol, Diane, and Steven, for accompanying me on many arduous photographic jaunts and for patiently allowing me the time to determine, assemble, and create the many items involved in the publication of this book.

ROBERT P. OLMSTED
Woodridge, Illinois
April 1975

AN ACQUAINTANCE WITH ALCOS

The American Locomotive Company (Alco Products) will be first in this book, since we are taking each diesel locomotive builder in alphabetical order. Observations of the popularity of various diesel-electric locomotive models with the railroad enthusiasts of this country would indicate that Alco holds first place from that standpoint too. It is not necessarily that Alco's locomotives were better; it seems to be a combination of pleasing design, and the fact that Alco produced fewer units, thus making them somewhat rare in the scheme of things.

Back in the days when steam was still "king of the rails," the three largest builders of locomotives were the American Locomotive Company, the Baldwin Locomotive Works, and the Lima Locomotive Works. Several railroads, notably the Pennsylvania Railroad and the Norfolk & Western, also built a considerable number of their own steam locomotives. The American Locomotive Company produced steam power from the 1850's until 1948. Alco also joined with General Electric in the design and construction of electric locomotives beginning early in this century. GE produced several diesel-electric locomotives in 1918, but they did not find railroads knocking on the door for products. In 1924, they produced another unit which met with considerably more success. General Electric, Ingersoll-Rand, and Alco combined to build a small number of diesel switchers during the next four years. Alco's contributions to this joint venture was the building of locomotive bodies. In addition, Alco produced three experimental locomotives in 1928 at the request of the New York Central. In 1929 the American Locomotive Company began building diesels on its own, although they continued to use the electrical equipment supplied by GE. Their first self-generated venture resulted in a yard switcher which went to the New Haven as their No. 0900 in 1931. The locomotive was followed by a standardized line of switchers sold as a catalog item and not custom built. During the 1930's over 100 switchers of varying shapes and power were delivered while the main effort of the Alco plant was still erecting steam locomotives such as Union Pacific's twenty-five giant 4-8-8-4's, known as the *Big Boy,* in the early 1940's.

In 1935 Alco engines were used to power the Gulf, Mobile & Northern's streamlined *Rebel* trains; and in 1936 Alco supplied the first turbocharger to a railroad diesel. Alco's first passenger unit, the DL109, appeared in 1940. This was a dual-engined unit developing 2000 h.p. out of two switcher engines and sold

first to the Rock Island as their No. 624. Between 1940 and 1953, Alco and GE combined their marketing forces under the banner of Alco-GE. Many of Alco's most popular diesel locomotives, such as the PA and the FA models, were constructed following World War II and carried this builder's plate.

During the World War II years, Alco's diesel production was restricted by the War Production Board, while General Motors continued to build freight diesel locomotives. The War Production Board felt the Alco plant was best suited to the construction of steam. Thus, at the end of the war, Electro-Motive Division of General Motors had a significant head start in its drive to replace steam with diesels. Also problems in Alco's early post-war locomotives didn't help post-war sales. The tables might possibly have been turned had Alco been permitted to build diesel freight units during the war years.

Alco generally receives credit for the first "road-switcher" design. The idea was to take the switcher, fit it with road trucks, upgrade the power unit if necessary, and use the resulting locomotive for branch line or way freight service. The versatility of this type of power soon took over the entire road locomotive market. The unit could be used by itself, or in multiple, or refined to handle almost any task on the mainline. Alco built a few units in 1941, with large numbers being produced beginning in 1946. EMD's first road-switchers came out in 1948-1949. The year 1951 turned out to be the peak in domestic diesel sales for Alco. After 1953, GE started off on its own to develop a complete line of road locomotives. The American Locomotive Co. continued with the manufacture of diesels, changing their corporate name to Alco Products in 1956. During the 1960's, Alco's share of the locomotive market gradually declined. For many years they had held the number two sales position, but gradually yielded that spot to General Electric. Alco's final production of new diesel locomotives took place in 1969 at its Schenectady, New York, plant. The Montreal Locomotive Works (for many years the Canadian subsidiary of Alco) purchased the Alco designs and agreements, and at this writing is still much in the locomotive business in Canada, building export diesels containing many of the Alco features.

Despite their departure from the field of diesel production in the United States, Alco's locomotives are still eagerly sought out by rail buffs; and their PA passenger locomotive is often considered the most popular diesel locomotive ever built.

Predecessor to the PA - DL109

The DL109 was Alco's first attempt at a diesel passenger locomotive. The dual-engines in the DL109 provided 2000 h.p., the same as that produced by competing General Motors E-units of 1939-1940. Of the 74 locomotives of this type built for U. S. railroads, the New York, New Haven & Hartford had sixty. Four booster units, the DL110, were also built. The various locomotives of this DL109 model weighed in the range of 325,000 to 355,000 lbs. New Haven DL109 0748 has just arrived in Springfield, Massachusetts from New Haven with a morning departure from New York in August 1954.

Santa Fe purchased one DL109 and one DL110 (the booster unit) from Alco. Numbered 50 and 50A, the units spent most of their service life on so-called "secondary" runs on the AT&SF, such as Chicago-Kansas City-Tulsa. Of course on the AT&SF the secondary runs were often more plush than many of the top trains on other railroads. *Upper Left* . . . Several miles out of Lawrence, Kansas, 50 heads Train 12, the *Chicagoan*, eastbound in January 1951. *Lower Left* . . . The engineer waits for a handful of passengers and a few sacks of mail as Number 12 makes a brief pause in Lawrence. 50 and an EMD "B" unit are providing the horses. 50 was built in May 1941 and scrapped in October 1960. *Above* . . . Gulf, Mobile & Ohio owned three DL109's. Two of the three, 270 and 272, are easing to a stop at the East St. Louis, Illinois station in 1952.

Roster of DL109 Locomotives (built early 1940 to mid 1945) . . .
AT&SF 50
CMSTP&P 14A, 14B
C&NW 5007A
CRI&P 621, 622, 623, 624
GM&O 270, 271, 272
NEW HAVEN 0700-0759
SOUTHERN (and subsidiaries) 2904, 6400, 6401
Total . . . 74 units

DL110 (boosters) . . . AT&SF 50A, SOUTHERN (and subsidiaries) 2954, 6425, 6426
Total . . . 4 units

(NOTE: Some sources indicate that CRI&P 624, listed in this section as the first DL109, should be considered a separate model because it differed somewhat in machinery arrangement and a few design features from subsequent DL109's)

New Haven 0758, *(Upper Left)* attired in green with yellow striping, roars through Thompsonville, Connecticut at 2:00 PM on an early November afternoon in 1954. *Lower Left* . . . 0752 and 0753 are departing Springfield, Massachusetts, with Train 75 on New Year's Day in 1955. Both of these locomotives were in the last group of New Haven DL109's (0750-0759) and were delivered in 1945 as railroad class DER-1c. *Below* . . . In Springfield, Massachusetts, the tracks run east-west through the station. New Haven trains bound south for New York and Boston & Maine trains bound north for White River Jct., Vermont, would sometimes stand side by side waiting for departure time. NH DL109 0717 and B&M EMD E7 3809 pause for a portrait in August 1954.

The New Haven used their sixty DL109's as dual-purpose locomotives, handling the many passenger runs during the day and freight hauls at night, thus getting extensive use out of the units. *Upper Left* . . . 0708 hustles into Springfield, Massachusetts, on a wintry mid-March day in 1956. *Lower Left* . . . New Haven's first group of DL109's (0700-0709) in railroad class DER-1a came in 1941-1942. 0700 waits for departure time in Springfield. Looks like the hunter's green paint on the nose could use a little touching up in this 1955 view. *Above* . . . The 0750 breezes through Windsor, Connecticut with the 5:15 PM departure from Springfield in 1955.

The first DL109 became Rock Island 624. Subsequently the CRI&P purchased 3 more in 1940-1941, their 621-623. *Below* . . . 621 makes a flag stop in Lawrence, Kansas, in May 1949. The 621 was repowered by EMD in mid-1953 altering the roof line but leaving the nose styling by Otto Kuhler relatively unchanged. 621 remained in the general passenger locomotive pool until 1968. 622-624 were scrapped in the early 1960's. *Left* . . . 621 on the *Peoria Rocket* at Englewood Station in Chicago. *Above* — Departing LaSalle from Roosevelt Road in Chicago in 1967.

PA's on the Santa Fe

Following up their pre-World War II DL109 design, the American Locomotive Company introduced a new passenger unit in mid-1946. Popularly called the PA, the first unit went to the Santa Fe. Forty-three more locomotives for the AT&SF followed between 1946 and 1948. During the winter of 1967-1968 the Santa Fe started using thirteen of their remaining Alco PA passenger diesels on Trains 23 and 24. As it was to turn out this was their final grand performance on the AT&SF. All except one of the following photographs in this section depict these final months. *Below . . .* PA's 67 and 71 curve past the depot in Coal City, Illinois, with Number 23. *Right . . .* 76 and 55 have just clattered through the AT&SF-GM&O junction at Pequot on the outskirts of Coal City with 23. The date of both photographs is January 1968. In late 1967 the Santa Fe sold four PA's (59, 60, 62, 66) to the Delaware & Hudson for use on their Albany-Montreal passenger trains. Renumbered D&H 16-19, these locomotives are the only PA type diesels to survive in 1975.

Number 23 hurries across the Des Plaines River near Lemont, Illinois, behind the red, yellow, and silver noses of 78 and 75 in February 1968. By the middle of February the Alco's had been replaced on 23 and 24 by EMD power for the last time. PA operators included: AT&SF; D&H; UP; Wabash; SP; Pennsy; NYC; Nickel Plate; Lehigh Valley; New Haven; M-K-T; MoPac; Erie (E-L); D&RGW; Southern; St. Louis Southwestern; and GM&O.

Above . . . 70 and 71 are easing down the leads to Dearborn Station in Chicago to lock couplers with the waiting consist of Number 23. *Below* . . . One PA and three cars comprise a very abbreviated eastbound Train 24 in Joliet, Illinois. The lone PA is 58 on this February 1968 afternoon. The rather leisurely schedule of 23 and 24 presented no particular problems for one or two PA's and on-time performance was normal.

Upper Left ... 71 and 67 and Number 23 drum across the ship canal adjacent to the Des Plaines River approaching Lemont, Illinois. *Lower Left* ... In January 1968 the 67 is waiting for a crew at the 18th Street servicing facilities in Chicago during a brisk snow squall off Lake Michigan. *Above* ... Back in May 1949, when the front ends of the Alco's were less cluttered, 70 breezes into Lawrence, Kansas, with the *Kansas Cityan*. EMD FT 166, regeared for passenger service, waits in the siding for Number 11 to clear before heading east. *Below* ... On one of the last passenger runs on the AT&SF to which the PA's were assigned, 68 is really rolling westward at Ransom, Illinois, with Number 23. The date is February 9, 1968.

Above . . . A set of EMD's F-units is backing into the 18th Street passenger locomotive servicing facilities of the Santa Fe in Chicago. PA 75 in the foreground will soon be moving to Dearborn Station for Number 23. In the distance an Illinois Central switcher clatters by with the Chicago skyline for a backdrop. *Right Above . . .* PA 76 is departing the Joliet station westbound on 23 and is just moving across the Rock Island mainline. *Right Below . . .* A few minutes before the departure time for the *Grand Canyon*, PA 78 rests in Chicago's Dearborn Station. After the PA's were removed from 23 and 24 they saw relatively little service on the Santa Fe. A few were used briefly in freight service in California and of course there was a farewell fan excursion. Alco's 58 and 67 handled the California excursion to mark the end of an era on the Santa Fe. The last remaining AT&SF PA's were being traded in for new power in March 1969. Because of its looks and general character, the PA is usually regarded as the most popular type of diesel locomotive built. If Alco Products was still in business, they might be getting an order now and then for a PA to serve on a tourist or excursion line!

RS27

In late 1959 American Locomotive Company introduced a 2400 h.p. freight locomotive given the model number RS27. Only 27 of the RS27's were built 1959-1962 before a new series, the Century 424, replaced it in the builder's catalog in 1963. A quite short nose with notches in the upper corners gives these units an unusual appearance when viewed from the front. A large one-piece windshield also contributes to the different look of these locomotives.

Soo Line's only two RS27's, (Left) 416 and 415, are moving a transfer run across Burlington Northern rails in Minneapolis only a block or two away from the Twin Cities Amtrak Station. Above . . . The Alco's are easing off the Soo's Mississippi River bridge at Camden Place in Minneapolis and are turning south with the daily transfer run to the C&NW. This run is the normal duty of the RS27's these days, although one of them will sometimes team with an EMD unit on other local runs in the Twin Cities area.

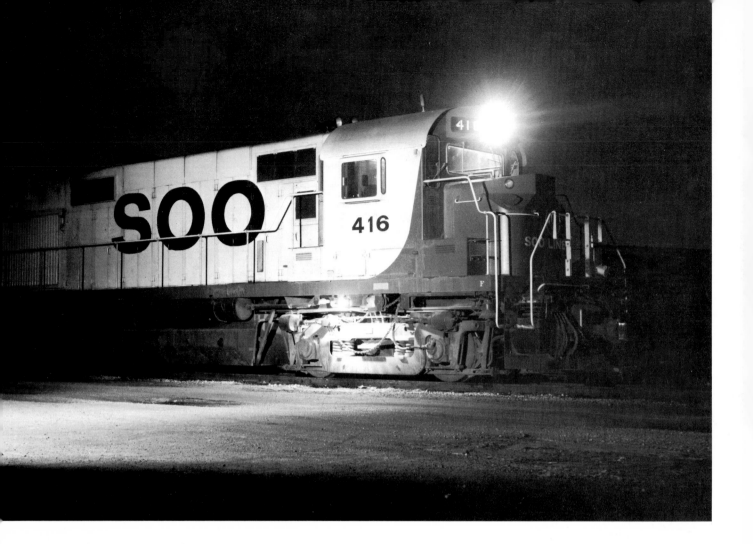

Upper Left . . . In the days before Soo 415 and 416 were restricted to local service in the Twin Cities area, the 416 is about to depart the ready track in Schiller Park, Illinois, in company with a GP30, to power a northbound freight. *Lower Left* . . . 415 eases beneath an overpass on its way to the C&NW's Railway Transfer Yard in Minneapolis. The Soo's two RS27's came in 1962. *Above* . . . At the end of the run 415 and 416 have just cut off their train and are about to head back to the north end of the yard for a return trip to the Soo's Shoreham Yard.

Below . . . The Pennsylvania Railroad owned the most RS27's, a modest fleet of 15, numbered 2400-2414. Here the 2400 is accelerating past a departing *South Wind* at Englewood Station in Chicago in May 1966.

Initially the Green Bay & Western owned just one of the RS27's, the 310 pictured here. The 310 came to the GB&W in 1960. After the C&NW traded their four 1962 built RS27's back to Alco in 1966, the GB&W acquired two of them in 1968. These two became Green Bay & Western 316 and 317. The RS27's generally weighed between 247,000 and 257,000 lbs. and were 57 feet long. *Below* . . . 310 and C424 311 are eastbound through Merrillan, Wisconsin, en route from Winona, Minnesota, to Green Bay. *Right* . . . GB&W 310 and 311 roll through snow covered farm land near Independence, Wisconsin in January 1973.

Roster of RS27 Locomotives (built late 1959 to late 1962)...
ALCO DEMONSTRATORS   640-1
                                      640-2, 640-3, 640-4, 640-5 (to UP as 675-678)
C&NW 900, 901, 902, 903 (902, 903 to GB&W 316, 317)
GB&W 310
PRR 2400-2414
SOO 415-416
Total . . . 27 units

Above ... At Fourth Ave. N. in Minneapolis, the Soo Line's two red and white RS27's are southbound with the "Railway Transfer". The long one-piece windshield is very noticeable from this overhead angle. *Upper Right* ... Green Bay & Western 310 is rolling right along near Taylor, Wisconsin, with the eastbound day freight for Green Bay. *Lower Right* ... About midway in their daily journey from Shoreham Yard to Railway Transfer, 416 and 415 are heading south through Minneapolis in November 1973. The successor to the 2400 h.p. RS27 in Alco's production line was the Century 424. Both models used the same 251B engine. External design differences can be seen by comparing the photographs in this section with those on the following pages.

Chicago's own C424's - Belt Railway Co.

When Alco Products brought forth its Century series in 1963, the 2400 h.p. model (replacing the RS27) was termed the Century 424. Fifty-three C424 locomotives were built for U.S. railroads 1963-1967. 424's were built for use in Canada and Mexico as well. The Belt Railway Company of Chicago ordered six C424's from Alco in 1965-1966. Numbered 600-605, these Alco's roam much of the Belt's Chicagoland trackage. Other U.S. operators of the C424 are: Burlington Northern (ex-SP&S); Erie-Lackawanna; Erie Mining; Green Bay & Western; Norfolk & Western (ex-Wabash); Penn Central (ex-PRR); Reading; and Toledo, Peoria & Western.

One of the regular assignments of the Belt Railway C424's has been the transfer runs to the North Western's Proviso Yard in the northwest suburbs of Chicago from the Belt's south side yard. The trip is made via Indiana Harbor Belt-Baltimore & Ohio Chicago Terminal trackage. *Above* . . . The return run from Proviso is a caboose hop as the 602 and 600 heading south clatter past Milwaukee Road's 63A northbound in Broadview, Illinois. Milwaukee Road trains to and from Indiana use IHB-B&OCT tracks for part of the trip. *Upper Right* . . . On a rainy May morning in 1969, Belt 605 and 601 are northbound through Bellwood with the transfer run to the C&NW. *Lower Right* . . . 600 and 603 are moving through Proviso Yard in September 1969. On flats behind the Alco's is steam locomotive 101 of the T. R. Miller Mill Company en route to a tourist line.

34

Northbound past McCook Tower on a crisp January morning, 600 is just a moment away from banging over the AT&SF mainline with the C&NW transfer.

Above . . . Belt Railway 604 grinds uphill through Bellwood. The Belt C424's are about 59 feet in length and weigh in near 272,000 lbs. The color scheme is a tasteful grey, yellow, and black with white lettering. *Right* . . . On a grim, grey Chicago morning, in contrast to the sunshine on the 604, 600 in about to duck under Roosevelt Road in Broadview, Illinois.

Above . . . Heading north, Belt 602 is emerging from beneath Burlington Route (now BN) rails in La Grange, Illinois. Usually a pair of Alco's are assigned but today the 602 is going it alone. *Below* . . . 600 rolls past an ex-Santa Fe caboose of the Indiana Harbor Belt in Bellwood on a bright February morning in 1973. *Right* . . . The Ogden Avenue bridge in La Grange provides an overhead view of the 600 and 603 northbound. Normally the transfer runs to Proviso Yard have used the westernmost track north of the Santa Fe crossing at McCook.

C628 on the North Western

In addition to the C424, Alco's Century series of 1963 featured a six-wheel truck, 2750 h.p. model termed the C628. The Norfolk & Western purchased high-nosed C628's in 1965 and 1966 and numbered them 1100-1129. Some of these Alco's were leased to and then all were sold to the Chicago & North Western in early 1973. The C&NW was in dire need of more power to handle an upsurge in traffic. 1100-1129 became 6701-6730 on the employee-owned C&NW. *Above . . .* 6715 rests beside SD45 905 in Union Yard, Minneapolis.

Above . . . Still in N&W blue with traces of the lettering still visible under a quick band of paint, C&NW 6711, ex-N&W 1110, faces an early morning autumn sun in Minneapolis. Below . . . Black 6708 and yellow 6725 are urging Train 490 out of Union Yard in Minneapolis during a January 1974 snow shower.

Left Above . . . On January 26, 1975 North Western 6724 leads three more 6700's and southbound freight out of Spooner, Wisconsin, on the run to Minneapolis. When received from the N&W some of the **Alco's** were blue and some were black; they are now repainted in the C&NW's familiar yellow and green. *Left Below* . . . At Westminster Tower (barely visible in the background) Train 490 curves through a triangular pattern of trackage heading toward Wisconsin. 6708 and 6725 power the consist in January 1974. *Above* . . . At Western Avenue in St. Paul, the pair of Alco's roll beneath the telltales.

Above . . . North Western 6724 is southbound near Turtle Lake, Wisconsin in January 1975. *Left* . . . At Clear Lake, Wisconsin, Chicago & North Western 6714-6720-6722 are heading for the Twin Cities during the late afternoon hours of a beautiful autumn day. *Below* . . . 6721 and 6706, in bright new yellow and green paint, are accelerating Train 462 away from New Richmond, Wisconsin with a combined 5500 h.p. The 69 foot long C628's carried a weight of about 405,000 lbs. Alco built 135 of the big Century 628's for U.S. railroads, but the ex-N&W units were the only high-nosed locomotives in the group. C628's are operated by the following U.S. railroads: Delaware & Hudson (18); Lehigh Valley (17, of which 9 are ex-Monon); Louisville & Nashville (15); C&NW (30); Penn Central (15, ex-PRR); Seaboard Coast Line (11, ex-ACL); and Southern Pacific (29, four of which are ex-demonstrators).

Upper Left ... North Western Train 462 thunders over the road leading to the Clear Lake, Wisconsin, golf course. It is mid-October though and golfing days are about over for the season in the north country. *Lower Left* ... Earlier in the afternoon, 6721 and 6706 move 462 through the pleasant Wisconsin countryside west of Deer Park. *Above* ... Right at sunset, three of the big Alco's roll westward with tonnage for the Twin Cities. 6714-6720-6722 are between Deer Park and New Richmond, Wisconsin, in October 1973.

Above . . . C628's 6721 and 6706 on Train 462 have just crossed the city limits from Minneapolis into St. Paul and are en route to Superior, Wisconsin. *Below* . . . The long clean lines of the C628 along with Alco's trademark notches in the corners of the roof line are evident as 6721-6706 roll through St. Paul. *Right* . . . At Northline Jct., the Superior line leaves the main leading toward Milwaukee and Chicago (track visible at left). 6721 and 6706 have been working hard the last few miles climbing out of the St. Croix River valley.

BUILT BY BALDWIN

The Baldwin Locomotive Works, like Alco and Lima, was a long time builder of steam locomotives. Their record of locomotive construction dates back to 1832 with the construction of *Old Ironsides*. Many railroads stayed with their favorite locomotive builder through thick and thin. As an example, a good many of the steam locomotives built for the Santa Fe Railway from World War I to the end of steam came from Baldwin. BLW began tinkering with experimental gasoline locomotives during the early years of the 20th century. They also trial tested a 1000 h.p. road diesel in 1925. This unit was considerably more powerful than the 300 and 600 h.p. diesels constructed by General Electric and Alco at about the same time period. After testing the unit on the Reading Railroad the unit was modified and later scrapped. Samuel Vauclain, the head of the Baldwin Locomotive Works, found the locomotive powerful enough, but still could not match the tractive effort of a steam locomotive of the same weight on drivers.

In 1936 Baldwin produced their first switcher with a De La Vergne engine. This was to be the only type engine used in Baldwin's production of diesels for some time. Variations in number of cylinders and in turbocharging came with various locomotive models, but the basic engine remained unchanged. By 1939 the Works was offering a line of switchers and had a line of road units under consideration as World War II intervened.

Baldwin, like the other locomotive builders, had its activities restricted during the war years. As a prime builder of steam locomotives, their efforts continued with the erection of steam power for the war effort. While they were permitted to continue their line of diesel switchers, the firm was not allowed to spend time developing prototype freight and passenger units for the future. It wasn't until 1945 that their first road diesel appeared.

In the meantime, General Motors had ironed out many of the "bugs" afflicting diesel locomotives and continued a research program all during the war years. Besides GM had a large sales force on the ground, a group with years of experience in the new car market. While Baldwin had a good product, their sales team was never able to crack GM's stranglehold in the traffic of diesel locomotives.

The Baldwin Locomotive Works had built steam locomotives for over 100 years and yet their production of road-type diesel locomotives lasted barely a decade.

Meanwhile, Electro-Motive Division's early passenger E-units and FT freighters, were rolling on many mainline railroads. While Baldwin was always willing to build a locomotive to a customer's order, GM was turning out diesel machines on an assembly line basis and at favorable prices. The Baldwin diesel locomotives were noted for their ability to take abuse, to stand-up to rough and rugged conditions, and for their capacity to lug heavy tonnage. Baldwin road units were not too numerous; but their switchers sold well, performed creditably, and a few are still at work in 1975 with far more miles racked up on their frames and traction motors than many GM units.

A merger with another small builder of diesels, Lima-Hamilton, failed to turn the tide, and in 1956 the last new locomotive left the Baldwin-Lima-Hamilton plant in Eddystone, Pennsylvania. A few experiments with lightweight trains followed with unfavorable results and Baldwin disappeared from the railroad field.

Sharknoses in Cincinnati - NYC RF16

In 1951 and 1952, the New York Central purchased eighteen 1600 h.p. cabs and eight companion booster units from the Baldwin Locomotive Works. These 18 cabs, numbered 3804-3821, featured the so-called "shark nose" design patterned after Pennsylvania Railroad steam and diesel passenger locomotives of the late 1940's. In addition to the NYC units, there were 72 cabs and 30 boosters built for the Pennsy and 19 cabs and 13 boosters for the Baltimore & Ohio, making a total RF16 production of 109 cabs and 51 "B" units. PRR and B&O also owned similar looking 1500 h.p. freight diesels of another model number (DR4-4-15).

During the summer of 1967 the remaining NYC "sharks", now renumbered 1204-1221, were in what was to turn out to be the last year of operation for most. The 1211 rests in a hot June 1967 sun in Cincinnati, Ohio.

Most of the still active NYC RF16's were assigned to transfer service between the Riverside Yard in Cincinnati and NYC's yard in Sharonville, Ohio, some sixteen miles north. Once in a while some would work north to Indianapolis as well as fill in on other transfer duties. *Above* ... 1213 and 1209 idle on a humid summer night in Sharonville. *Upper Right* ... 1205 and 1204 are northbound through Cincinnati en route to Sharonville early on what will soon become a hot summer day in Ohio. *Lower Right* ... The 1215 basks in the last rays of sun in Cincinnati in company with NYC switchers 8106 and 8107.

52

Upper Left ... On a quiet Sunday afternoon, 1204 and 1205 loaf in Cincinnati. *Lower Left* ... In a time exposure at dawn, 1215-1217 wait for a seemingly endless train of hoppers to clear before picking up their train in the Sharonville yard. *Above* ... Bursting out from beneath a viaduct, NYC Baldwin 1205 flushes out several birds from the tall grass beside the tracks. The "shark" is nearing Sharonville.

New York Central's Baldwin RF16's were listed as railroad class DFA-8a and weighed in at about 255,000 lbs. each. As with most Baldwin diesels, they were known as good heavy tonnage engines-rugged and dependable. *Above* . . . Throbbing away on the ready track, 1205-1204 wait for a crew and another transfer drag. *Right* . . . At the Sharonville diesel facility, 1217 and an EMD F-unit stand under the sanding and fueling racks.

Above . . . From an overhead angle, the rounded roof lines of the RF16 are evident as 1205 and 1204 ease up to the south end of Sharonville's yard. *Right* . . . 1207 stares into a bay of the diesel shop in Sharonville in June 1967. By September the Baldwins were being traded in by the New York Central after about fifteen years of service. 1207 got a temporary reprieve though. Along with 1205, 1209, 1213, 1216, and 2 "B" units, the 1207 went to the Monongahela Railway in southwestern Pennsylvania for a few more years of occasional service. By early 1974 only the 1205 and the 1216 survived on the Monongahela roster. These last two RF16's now have been purchased by the Delaware & Hudson Railway, which you will recall also operates the last remaining Alco PA's. Credit for continuing preservation of these historic types of locomotives goes to enthusiastic D&H President, Carl B. Sterzing, Jr.

Double-enders East-Jersey Central Lines

Baldwin's passenger diesel locomotives were essentially custom built. Each railroad purchaser was supplied with a somewhat differing appearance to its units. To avoid the problem of turning the locomotives around, the Central Railroad of New Jersey wanted diesels with a cab at each end for their suburban service. Baldwin constructed six units in this manner for the CNJ, numbered 2000-2005. *Below* . . . On a summer Sunday in 1954, Jersey Central 2000 idles on the point of its commuter consist waiting for the Monday morning rush. The railroad class for these six locomotives was PD-30. The scene is at Bay Head, New Jersey.

2002 hustles Train 3357 through South Amboy, New Jersey en route from New York to Bay Head. 2000-2002 came from Baldwin in 1946-1947 followed by 2003-2005 in 1948. Different side panels appeared on the second group as can be seen in the photographs. Delivered in a blue and orange color scheme, the Baldwins wore an olive green with yellow stripes in these 1954-1955 photos. The units weighed a hefty 383,500 lbs. each.

Upper Left . . . 2005 races commuters to New York early on a May morning in 1955. The Baldwin is near Morgan, New Jersey, beside the waters of Raritan Bay. *Lower Left* . . . Beneath the catenary used by Pennsylvania Railroad GG-1's, CNJ 2004 hurries six cars through South Amboy toward New York City. *Above* . . . 2001 spends a November 1955 Sunday at Bay Head. *Below* . . . The first of CNJ's DR6-4-20 locomotives, number 2000, heads commuters home along the sandy shores of Raritan Bay between South Amboy and Morgan. The dual-engined 2000 h.p. locomotives could be considered comparable to Alco's DL109 and EMD's early E-units as Baldwin's diesel experience was still limited in the mid 1940's.

Under the signal bridge at the end of the PRR catenary (where GG-1's were exchanged for a K4s in those steam days on the Pennsy), 2004 has at least twelve cars of holiday travelers headed for Jersey beaches. The date is Saturday, July 2, 1955, and a long weekend is ahead.

Upper Right . . . Minneapolis, Northfield & Southern Baldwin center cab 21 is about to pick up a transfer run in the MN&S yard in Golden Valley, a Minneapolis suburb. *Lower Right* . . . At Medicine Lake Road between Golden Valley and New Hope, Minnesota, 21 is en route to the Burlington Northern's Northtown Yard in January 1974.

Roster of DT6-6-20 Locomotives (built 1948-1950) . . .
AT&SF 2600-2606
DSS&A 300-303 (to SOO 396-399)
EJ&E 101-126
MN&S 20-24
SSW 260
TRONA 50, 51 (to PEABODY COAL CO.)
Total . . . 45 units
(Note: EJ&E 100 built 1946 was somewhat similar non-turbocharged version)

In August 1972, Minneapolis, Northfield & Southern's Baldwin transfer unit number 21 was attending to its usual duties. *Upper Right* . . . 21 is working in the MN&S yard; and in the other two photographs the blue Baldwin heads south from Golden Valley, on the west edge of Minneapolis, with a transfer drag. The Minnesota shortline received five of the Baldwin DT6-6-20's, numbered 20-24, in 1948. Weighing in at about 355,000 lbs., the units are 74 feet in length and develop 2000 h.p. out of two 1000 h.p. engines, one in each end of the locomotive. Forty-five units of this type were built by Baldwin. The largest group went to the Elgin, Joliet & Eastern. Of the five locomotives owned by the MN&S, 20, 22, and 24 were scrapped between 1966 and late 1968. The 23 had been stored for some time and was sold for scrap early in 1974. The 21 was retired from service in late summer 1974.

In January 1974 the sole active DT6-6-20 of the MN&S was still the 21. *Left Above* ... 21 and caboose roll across the Soo Line's Mississippi River bridge en route to the BN's Northtown Yard in Minneapolis. *Left Below* ... 21 is coming off MN&S rails onto Soo iron at Soo Junction in New Hope with cars for the Soo's Humboldt Yard. *On This Page* ... After setting out a Soo box on a New Hope siding, 21 drifts back to its train. In the overhead view the big Baldwin is northbound through New Hope.

LOCOMOTIVES FROM LA GRANGE

The Electro-Motive Division of General Motors Corporation (EMD) has reigned as the number one builder of diesel-electric locomotives since the mid-1940's.

As a beginning to this remarkable record, the reader must go back to 1922 when an Harold Hamilton set up a company to sell gas-electric rail cars. This sales firm, the Electro-Motive Corporation, initially had no manufacturing facility of its own. The Winton Engine Company produced the engines to their design and Pullman and other firms built frames and car bodies. EMC was fairly successful in their sales effort against General Electric competition.

In 1930 General Motors purchased EMC as well as the Winton Engine Company. These firms remained subsidiaries of General Motors for about ten years. EMC continued to build gas-electric cars throughout the mid-1930's.

The debut in 1934 of the first streamlined trains catapulted the Electro-Motive Division's predecessor company into the position of front-runner in the field of railroad streamlining with Winton engines powering both pioneer trains. Burlington's *Zephyr* was equipped with a diesel engine, while Union Pacific's *City of Salina* contained a distillate engine. The articulated car bodies were built by Budd and Pullman respectively.

It should be remembered that General Electric and the American Locomotive Company had been producing diesel powered switchers prior to EMC's installing a diesel engine in the *Zephyr*. EMC continued to encourage railroads to enter the streamliner market, and several more articulated streamlined trains for the Union Pacific and the Burlington were equipped with EMC's motors. The Boston & Maine's *Flying Yankee* of 1935 also contained an EMC-Winton engine.

The year 1935 was a big one for Electro-Motive. In that year EMC designed two 1800 h.p. box-cab type road locomotives around their Winton diesel engines. Numbered 511 and 512, they were erected at General Electric's Erie facility. These units toured the nation in order to acquaint railroad men and the general public with the superiority of the diesel locomotive over steam. In this same year, three diesel switchers were built for EMC, two went to the Delaware, Lackawanna & Western (their 425 and 426) and one was retained by EMC for a demonstrator as their No. 518. Ground was also broken on a new locomotive construction facility on the far west side of Chicago, near La Grange, Illinois. This site, vastly expanded of course, remains as GM's main assembly plant of diesel locomotives.

Locomotive construction began at their La Grange plant in 1936. During the late 1930's diesel-electric passenger locomotives were first built there. Many of these will be detailed in the accompanying section. In 1938 EMC started production of a new engine, the 567, and to build its own traction motors and electrical equipment instead of using parts from General Electric. Now EMC had taken over all facets of new locomotive construction in its own plant.

The first mass-produced diesel designed for road freight service was constructed in 1939 by EMC as its FT model. The four unit demonstrator, numbered 103, toured the nation's railroads and logged more than 80,000 miles handling every type of freight haul. The great success of this locomotive placed EMC solidly in the lead in diesel production and sales. The Santa Fe purchased the first fleet of FT's; and the initial revenue run began on February 4, 1941, as No. 100 rolled west out of Kansas City.

In 1941, the Electro-Motive Corporation and the Winton Engine Company were merged into General Motors to become the Electro-Motive Division of GM or better known as EMD. During World War II many freight diesels were built by EMD; and following the war, the firm held the position of leadership and has maintained it ever since. The competition was never able to obtain a marketing edge in order to overtake EMD's number one position.

The 50th anniversary of the original company was held in 1972, and an advertisement indicated that 37,154 diesel locomotives had been built to that date. When considering the number of diesel locomotives built to 1972, EMD has produced from 50 to 70 percent of all diesel locomotives erected, and in a few cases nearly 80 percent of the marketable units, within a given year. In recent years La Grange has completed nearly five units per day. The total locomotive production of GM reached well over 40,000 units during 1974.

Electro-Motive has produced such a wide variety of power that only a few can be illustrated here. The ones chosen are not their most popular models in terms of units constructed, but are selected to show a variety of shapes, and in some instances are actually quite rare in number.

Slanted noses for the streamliners

Following their first two non-articulated passenger units of 1935, Electro-Motive produced about 40 more early streamlined diesels between 1935 and mid-1938. These units were essentially customized for each purchaser although built around the Winton engine. In 1938 though, EMC came out with its new 567 engine and started in the business of mass-producing locomotives — beneath the paint the same locomotive for each railroad! The last traces of individualism included CB&Q 9908 *(Above*, departing St. Louis) which had one 1000 h.p. 567 engine and the last "shovel nose". The 9908 was built in April 1939. The standardized 2000 h.p. dual-engined diesels in E3, E4, E5, and E6 model numbers were known as "slant nosed" E-units. *Below* . . . CB&Q E5 9912A accelerated north from Savanna, Illinois, with the *Morning Zephyr* in 1960 as fan trip steam locomotive 5632 stands aside.

The Santa Fe slant nosed fleet totaled five cabs, E3 number 11 and four E6's 12-15, plus four booster units (11A, 12A, 13A, 15A). *Above* ... In January 1951 the 1939-built E3 leads the ten cars of the *Chicagoan* into Lawrence, Kansas. *Left* ... On the single track line west from Holliday through Topeka, Kansas, 11 barrels past a signal bridge with Train 11, the *Kansas Cityan*, near Wilder. *Right* ... On New Year's Day 1967, Second 19, the *Chief*, departs Dearborn Station in Chicago. Note the roof mounted bells on the AT&SF slant nosed diesels.

Illinois Central E6 4001 brakes to a quick stop in East St. Louis in September 1952. The IC roster included five E6 cabs, 4000-4004. The 4001 survived, in somewhat altered appearance, until the advent of Amtrak passenger service in 1971.

Roster of E3, E4, E5, and E6 locomotives . . .

E3A (built mid 1938 to mid 1940) . . . AT&SF 11; ACL 500; C&NW 5001A, 5002A;
CRI&P 625, 626; FEC 1001, 1002; KCS 1, 2, 3; MP 7000, 7001; UP LA-5
(to UP 5M-1A to UP 991).   *Total . . .* 14 units.

E3B . . . AT&SF 11A; C&NW 5001B, 5002B; UP LA-6.   *Total . . .* 4 units.

E4A (built 1938-1939) . . . SAL 3000-3013.   *Total . . .* 14 units.

E4B . . . SAL 3100-3104.   *Total . . .* 5 units.

E5A (built 1940-1941) . . . CB&Q 9909, 9910A, 9911A, 9912A, 9913, 9914A, 9914B,
9915A, 9915B; CB&Q (C&S) 9950A; CB&Q (FW&D) 9980A. *Total . . .* 11 units.

E5B . . . CB&Q 9910B, 9911B, 9912B; C&S 9950B; FW&D 9980B. *Total . . .* 5 units.

E6A (built late 1939 to September 1942) . . . AT&SF 12-15; ACL 501-523 (to SCL);
B&O 52, 57-63; C&NW 5004A, 5005A, 5005B, 5006A, 5006B; CMSTP&P 15A, 15B;
CRI&P 627-631; FEC 1003-1005; IC 4000-4004; KCS 24, 25; L&N 450A-457A
and 450B-457B; MP 7002, 7003; SAL 3014-3016; SR 2800-2802, 2900-2903;
UP LA-4, 7M-1A, 7M-2A, 8M-1A, 8M-2A, 9M-1A, 9M-2A.   *Total . . .* 92 units

E6B . . . AT&SF 12A, 13A, 15A; ACL 750-754; B&O 57X-63X; FEC 1051; MP 7002B,
7003B; SR 2950-2953; UP SF-5, SF-6, LA-5, LA-6.   *Total . . .* 26 units
(Note: UP renumbered units a number of times. As used in this section 993 was
originally 7M-2A and 996 was originally 9M-1A.)

On the Rock Island roster were two E3's, the 625 and 626, and five E6's, 627-631. *Upper Left* . . . Eight cars of the *Texas Rocket* move away from a flag stop in Lawrence, Kansas, behind the 627 in early 1952. *Lower Left* . . . On a cold December morning 626 stands across the Rock Island-Pennsy diamond at Englewood in Chicago. *Below* . . . Possibly the most famous E6 would be Rock Island's 630 if for no other reason than it was still in service into 1974. How much of the original locomotive remains after 30 years of duty is always an interesting question. In the case of the 630 the outward appearance changed little over the years although many different paint schemes were applied. In August 1966 the 630, in suburban service, waits to return to Chicago as E3 626 rolls into Joliet on the point of the *Golden State*.

Louisville & Nashville E6 776, built as the 456B in 1942, heads C&EI-L&N Train 93, the combined *Hummingbird* and *Georgian*, in October 1966. *Right* . . . At Dearborn Station in Chicago ready for departure, and *above*, 776 and trailing units are rounding the curve at 21st Street and heading south. *Below* . . . Seaboard Coast Line 514 (ex-Atlantic Coast Line 514 built in 1941) pauses at Englewood in Chicago with *The South Wind* in February 1968.

Above . . . Union Pacific E6 996 and two booster units roar across the Wyoming plains east of Cheyenne with the *City of Portland* in June 1952. *Lower Right* . . . In a more sedate roll in November 1952, the 996 heads the Kansas City-Salina local in Lawrence, Kansas, as UP 4-8-4 803 drifts past with its eastbound counterpart. *Below* . . . It is June 1951 and Union Pacific 993 and three "B" units are thundering upgrade on the long climb up Sherman Hill with the *City of Portland* westbound. *Upper Right* . . . Train 10, the *City of St. Louis*, has UP's lone E3 cab 991 in the lead in Lawrence, Kansas. 991 started life in March 1939 as LA-5 and is still around today, although hardly recognizable. It was rebuilt to an E9 in 1956 and renumbered 901. Then in 1969 it went to the Rock Island becoming their 663 where it can be seen in Chicagoland suburban service at this writing in 1975.

Above . . . Chicago & North Western 5004A (a 1941 E6) is westbound out of Laramie, Wyoming, on a "Cities" Streamliner in August 1951. The Chicago, Burlington & Quincy owned all sixteen of the E5's built. The E5 was really an E6 but covered with stainless steel panels at CB&Q request. All sixteen were built in 1940 and 1941 and each locomotive was named by the Q. *Below* . . . In their later years (1962-1964), with names removed from the side panels, 9915B *Silver Clipper* eases down the leads to Union Station in Chicago; and *Upper Right* . . . 9912A *Silver Meteor* accelerates the *California Zephyr* out of Union. *Lower Right* . . . In suburban Hinsdale, Illinois, CB&Q fan trip steamer 4960 waits as the 9912A passes on the three track main with the *Morning Zephyr*.

The Illinois Central purchased five E6 type diesels from EMC. Two of them, the 4001 and 4003 survived in IC service until Amtrak became the passenger operator in 1971. These units were extensively rebuilt during their 30 years of service however. *Above* . . . 4003 has just arrived at the IC station in Chicago in August 1964. *Upper Right* . . . In August 1960, a westbound freight behind 9226 holds at Broadview, Illinois, for 4003 and the *Land O'Corn* from Iowa. *Lower Right* . . . During March 1970 the 4001 bounds under a signal bridge just north of Monee, Illinois, with Number 8, the *Illini*.

The Baltimore & Ohio's E6 cabs were numbered 52 and 57-63 (52 replaced an earlier B&O passenger diesel transferred to the Alton). They were later renumbered 1407-1414 and were rebuilt to E8 rating of 2250 h.p. In these 1964-1966 photographs at Grand Central Station in Chicago, the rebuilding has already taken place but the slant noses remain. *Upper Left* . . . 1410 waits for a 10:15 PM departure with the *Diplomat*. 1411 and 1409 have arrived with inbound trains from the east and are about to head for the servicing facilities of the B&O in Chicago. B&O also owned seven E6B booster units 57X-63X which were renumbered in the 2400's and also rebuilt to E8 rating.

Through the doorway of a Rock Island suburban car in Joliet, Illinois, the yellow nose of E6 630 and a portion of the impressive station are visible. This was the paint scheme the 630 wore in August 1968.

Above . . . With a gold and red slant nose to go with its silver side panels, the 630 heads a 1972 excursion marking EMD's 50th anniversary. The *Golden Rocket* splits the signals near Putnam, Illinois, northbound on September 10th.

The gold nose still adorned the 630 in August 1973 as the last remaining active E6 continued in suburban service on the CRI&P.

FT - The first diesel freighters

The 100 — Santa Fe's first FT and the first FT to enter revenue service (February 4, 1941) stands at the Argentine (Kansas City, Kansas) engine facilities in July 1950. *Above . . .* A three unit set of FT's led by the 100 drones around a curve near Zarah, Kansas, with an eastbound freight in August 1951. The 100 has had its blue and yellow paint scheme revamped in the year between photographs. The first revenue FT was traded in to EMD in December 1956 for a GP9.

Above . . . An A-B-B set of FT's hustles westbound Santa Fe tonnage through Ottawa Junction, Kansas, in 1952. 184, in the lead, was formerly 173C built in 1945 and renumbered in June 1947. *Upper Right* . . . Back-to-back FT "A" units led by 199 roll westward into Lawrence, Kansas, in January 1952 with a short train. 199 was traded for a GP30 in February 1963. *Lower Right* . . . Keddie, California — more famous for its wye and trestles than its station-hosts Western Pacific FT 909D in 1965. The 1944 built 909D was one of 48 FT's on the WP in railroad class D-225. After more than twenty years of working tonnage through the Feather River Canyon, 909D was traded in on GP40's delivered in 1967.

Roster of FT operators in the U. S. . . . 1096 locomotives built late 1939 to late 1945.

FTA...AT&SF	155 units.	FTB...AT&SF	165 units.	FTA...MILW	26 units.	FTB...MILW	26 units.
ACL	24 "	ACL	24 "	MSTL	4 "	MSTL	2 "
B&O	12 "	B&O	12 "	MP	12 "	MP	12 "
B&M	24 "	B&M	24 "	NYC	4 "	NYC	4 "
CB&Q	32 "	CB&Q	32 "	NYO&W	9 "	NYO&W	9 "
C&NW	4 "	C&NW	4 "	NP	22 "	NP	22 "
CRI&P	20 "	CRI&P	16 "	RDG	10 "	RDG	10 "
DL&W	12 "	DL&W	8 "	SR	38 "	SR	30 "
D&RGW	24 "	D&RGW	24 "	SSW	10 "	SSW	10 "
ERIE	12 "	ERIE	12 "	SAL	22 "	SAL	22 "
GN	51 "	GN	45 "	WP	24 "	WP	24 "
LV	4 "	LV	4 "	Total . . . FTA	555 "	Total . . . FTB	541 "

(Note: totals for SR include Southern proper and its subsidiaries.)

After the Santa Fe's huge 320 locomotive FT fleet, Great Northern had the second largest group-96 units. In the winter of 1960-1961 GN FT's were working into Chicago on the Burlington Route. 401A and 424A . . . *Above* and *Upper Left* . . . stand in the Q's Clyde Yard diesel facilities. *Lower Left* . . . In another out of place posing, CB&Q 111A moves eastbound freight through Lawrence, Kansas, on UP rails in April 1952. Burlington trains were rerouted because of flood waters in Nebraska. Sixty-four of the diesel freighters worked for the CB&Q.

Forty-eight FT growlers appeared on the roster of the Boston & Maine. Delivered in 1943-1944, they were traded in on GP9's in 1957, a relatively short service life. During May 1955 B&M 4214 leads a freight through the mountains of western Massachusetts. The units have just crossed the Connecticut River near East Deerfield on the line through Hoosac Tunnel to Boston. The average FT weighed in the order of 230,000 to 240,000 lbs., and was about 48 feet long, and each unit developed 1350 h.p. The four portholes along the side of the FT was a common identifying characteristic, although in later years the FT's of some roads had these side panels changed.

Above ... 4210 and three companion FT's are resting between assignments in White River Junction, Vermont, in June 1954. The B&M color scheme during these years was red with yellow striping and a black pilot. *Below* ... 4200 and an FT "B" are heading for Boston at Billerica, Massachusetts, with three suburban cars in tow in the summer of 1954.

Upper Left . . . Rock Island FT 99 stands in the passing track in Lawrence, Kansas, with eastward tonnage at 11:00 PM on a January 1951 night. *Lower Left* . . . Eastbound CRI&P 4-8-4 5055 meets westbound freight behind FT 95 in Lawrence in December 1950. *Above* . . . B&M 4203 is about ready to depart Springfield, Massachusetts, northbound on the morning of June 12, 1956. *Below* . . . The Delaware, Lackawanna & Western 4050 h.p. A-B-A set of FT's is working through Binghampton, New York, on a grey March day in 1955.

Above . . . With the Kansas River (or Kaw, if your prefer) in the background, AT&SF 130 and an FT "B" move west out of Lawrence in early 1951. *Below* . . . During May 1951 the 109 leads three FT booster units and eastward freight down the Santa Fe main east of Ottawa, Kansas. Left hand running is the rule here. For the records the last remaining FT unit on the AT&SF turned out to be booster 429B which was traded to EMD in 1966. Of the 1096 locomotives built in FT configuration for U. S. railroads, three survive in 1974. Southern 6100, formerly one unit of the original demonstrator of 1939, is on display in St. Louis. One cab and one booster continue on the roster of Mexico's Sonora-Baja California (ex-NP units). The FT . . . surely a monumental locomotive of the diesel years!

On a branch line in Wisconsin - SDL 39

Above . . . North of Westby, Wisconsin, SDL39 581 of the Milwaukee Road heads north on the branch from Viroqua. Milwaukee's ten SDL39's are numbered 581-590. *Below* . . . 581 passes the tiny shelter at Melvina, Wisconsin, on a cold winter day. Surprisingly there is little snow on the ground here in mid-January.

On Tuesdays and Saturdays (at least at the time of these photographs), the Milwaukee Road's local freight east out of La Crosse, Wisconsin, turned south at Sparta for a run down the branch line to Viroqua. An SDL39 was not normally assigned, but here on January 20, 1973 the 581 handles the job. On the northward run 581 is between Cashton and Melvina, left and on this page. The 2300 hp. SDL39 was designed for the many light rail branches of this country. Considerably lighter and shorter than today's other road locomotives, the SDL has, so far, sold only to the Milwaukee (five in 1969 and five in 1972).

Left ... At Sparta Junction on the outskirts of Sparta, Wisconsin, the 581 is about to cross the C&NW heading north. *Above* ... The shortened length of the SDL is readily apparent as 581 clatters along beside the road just south of Cashton, Wisconsin. *Below* ... In a valley among Wisconsin's rolling hills, 581 scoots past through the frozen countryside. The SDL39 appears here because it is unique; and yet the general appearance of the unit (except for length) is characteristic of most EMD locomotives of the so-called "second generation" (from the GP35 and SD35 of late 1963-early 1964 onward).

F45/FP45 in Illinois

The F45/FP45s pictured in this section are the standard 3600 h.p. SD45 machinery with a non-structural cowling. The idea was to better protect the equipment and also the walkways along the side at speed. Santa Fe was the instigator of this design feature and assigned the first units (9 FP45's, 100-108) to the *Super Chief.* The units were renumbered to 5940-5948 in the general renumbering of 1969-1970. AT&SF also took delivery of forty F45 locomotives (no steam generator for passenger service) numbered 1900-1939 and renumbered 5900-5939. These F45's are about 68 feet long versus about 72 feet for the FP45. *Below* . . . 5948 on Train 2, the *San Francisco Chief*, is unloading passengers at Joliet, Illinois, in February 1971 as the westbound *Super Chief* departs on the right. *Upper Right* . . . Santa Fe's *Super C* behind 5928 pauses briefly in Joliet as the Amtrak *Chief* departs westward. *Lower Right* . . . 107 hammers the Chicagoland junction of Nerska with an eastbound freight in early 1968.

Nearly new 106 and 105 of the Santa Fe are breaking in on a freight haul in January 1968 as they cant to the curve in Lemont, Illinois. The FP's are dressed in the familiar red, yellow, and silver of AT&SF passenger locomotives. The F45's came in blue and yellow. *Right* . . . F45 5926 and an FP45 stand in a light snowfall in Joliet as passengers board Number 17, the *Super Chief/El Capitan.* F45's weighed in the order of 390,000 lbs. versus 410,000 for the four foot longer FP45.

Roster of FP45 Locomotives (built 1967-1968)...
AT&SF 100-108   (renumbered 5940-5948)
CMSTP&P 1-5
Total . . . 14 units

Roster of F45 Locomotives (built 1968-1971)...
AT&SF 1900-1939   (renumbered 5900-5939)
BN 6600-6613   (ex-GN 427-440)
BN 6614-6625   (ordered by GN as 441-452, delivered to BN)
BN 6626-6645
Total . . . 86 units

BN 6639 is heading west on the St. Paul line approaching Big Rock, Illinois, in 1971.

The Burlington Northern inherited a group of Great Northern F45's in the 1970 merger. BN then ordered twenty more which were delivered in 1971 making a total of 46 F45 locomotives. 6600-6613 were ex-GN 427-440 built in 1969. 6614-6625 were delivered as BN units after being ordered by the Great Northern. *Above* . . . At Eola, Illinois, BN 6623 is pumping up the air after a set out as BN 1579 and 6054 move up a yard track in the background. *Below* . . . Train 97 roars past the old red frame CB&Q depot in Shabbona, Illinois, behind BN 6640 in June 1972. Note the differing headlight placement on 6623 and 6640.

Upper Left . . . Racing east over the Illinois prairies, Burlington Northern 6628 is about to bombard a C&NW branch line a mile or so east of Shabbona. *Lower Left* . . . Down the center track of BN's three-track main, 6640 heads west in Eola, on the outskirts of Aurora, Illinois. *Below* . . . Cascade green BN 6639 and Big Sky blue BN 6613 (ex-GN 440) lean into a curve at Big Rock, Illinois in August 1971.

The lowest numbers possible were assigned to Milwaukee Road's five FP45's-numbers 1 to 5. *Left* . . . 2 and 1 are waiting to couple on the combined "Cities" train at Union Station in Chicago as 35C heads in on Train 46 in April 1969. *Above* . . . Milwaukee Road 3 is outbound from Union in February 1969. With the coming of Amtrak in 1971, Milwaukee's FP's were moved to freight duty and changed their yellow garb for the freight orange and black. *Below* . . . Great Northern 433 and 436 draw the lead assignment on BN 97 a few days after the GN-NP-CB&Q-SP&S merger of March 1970.

FM - THE OPPOSED PISTON PEOPLE

Fairbanks-Morse is another company which traces its origin back to before the middle of the last century. The Fairbanks Company, as it was then known, was not a builder of locomotives. The firm specialized in scales, and gradually expanded into railroad track scales, then eventually a number of other railroad supply items. The company began experimenting with gasoline engines and then all types of electric motors before and after the turn-of-the-century.

In the early 1930's Fairbanks-Morse developed an extremely successful opposed-piston diesel engine for submarine service. Several experiments with this engine in railroad use followed, particularly a switcher locomotive for the Reading Railroad in 1939. During the same year, an FM opposed-piston type engine was used to power six railcars for the Southern Railway. Preliminary designs for a line of road locomotives and switchers was on the firm's drawing boards when the nation began to prepare for war in 1940.

World War II postponed any research and development of locomotives until 1943. Near the end of the war years, FM made a strong bid for the diesel locomotive business. By early 1944, switchers were being constructed in FM's Beloit, Wisconsin, plant. The first engine was a 1000 h.p. unit built for the Milwaukee Road (No. 1802, later No. 760) which rolled forth on August 8, 1944.. The road units were built at General Electric's Erie, Pennsylvania, facility under contract from 1944 to 1949. These initial road units were often referred to as "Eries," due to the location of their erection. After 1949, all locomotive construc-

tion took place at Fairbanks-Morse's own plant.

The *Train Master,* a high performance 2400 h.p. hood unit was first introduced in 1953. The engine was far ahead of its competition at the time. Both Electro-Motive and Alco were offering units of less than 2000 h.p. Fairbanks-Morse promoted the unit on all fronts, for it soon realized it had a good product as railroads were interested in more power per unit. Unfortunately for FM, troubles developed in earlier FM units, and motive power officials of various railroads were rather reluctant to experiment with the *Train Master* until it had proven itself. By 1955 EMD and Alco had dieselized a major portion of America's railroads and new locomotive sales tended to level out. Between 1953 and 1956 Fairbanks was able to sell only 105 *Train Master* units in the United States and 22 in Canada, a true disappointment for a successful locomotive design. The *TM* did force its competition to come up with a comparable unit, but no *Train Master* sales were recorded after 1956.

Two lightweight trains were produced by Fairbanks-Morse in 1957-1958 with a locomotive unit on each end, one for the New Haven, and another for the Boston & Maine. The railroad builder constructed its final locomotive for an American carrier in 1958, although it continued to build locomotives for Mexico until 1963. The firm continued to supply parts and rebuild units since that time. With standardization still on the increase in 1975, i.e. ranks of SD40-2's, U30C's, and GP38-2's, it is interesting to dwell on the hopes for a new locomotive from Beloit.

114

C-Liners on the Milwaukee Road

The Consolidation Line of locomotives offered by Fairbanks-Morse included the CFA-16-4, a 1600 h.p. freight cab unit and the CFB-16-4 booster unit. The Milwaukee Road ordered eighteen locomotives of the C-Line (A-B-A sets, 23A-23B-23C through 28A-28B-28C). *Above* ... The first unit, 23A, is waiting for a refill of sand in Bensenville, Illinois. *Below* ... 24A moves out of Bensenville's yard with a long freight, both views were photographed in 1966.

Left . . . Bathed in the horizontal rays of an early morning sun in late October, 25A stands at the east end of Bensenville Yard. *Above* . . . The *Southeastern* trains to Indiana were one of the regular assignments of the C-Liners. 27C waits for the moment of departure in November 1966. *Below* . . . Milwaukee 37C bounds past with a train for Chicago as 25C waits to follow on a bitter December 1962 day in Milwaukee, Wisconsin.

Above . . . 23C at the Bensenville locomotive washer in 1966 and heading the *Southeastern* in 1965. *Right* . . . In Harvey, Illinois, 26C is doing some local work on the southward run to Indiana. Box car door openings provide the frame for this August 1966 scene.

C-Liners in model CFA-16-4 were ordered in the U.S. by the Milwaukee, New York Central, and the Pennsylvania Railroad, and were built 1950-1953. Thirty-six cabs (plus eighteen CFB boosters) comprised the total production of this model for U.S. roads. *Above* . . . Only a few months before it was silenced forever, 1951-built 28C waits in a drizzling rain for servicing in the company of EMD 69C. The 69C was built in 1950 and was still in service through 1973. The FM's were gone in 1967. *Upper Right* . . . 27C pokes its nose out of the Bensenville diesel shop in 1966. *Lower Right* . . . The *Southeastern* gets out of Bensenville behind the 24A, an EMD "B" unit, and another FM, as a "Cities" Streamliner glides by in the background. 24A wears the newer orange and black color scheme. The *Southeastern's* name comes from the Chicago, Terre Haute & Southeastern Railroad, now part of the Milwaukee Road.

Left . . . FM 25A throbs along past the caboose track in the low sun of early morning in October. *Below* . . . Also still in the older maroon and orange paint scheme, the 24C stands amid snow banks in Bensenville in January 1967. Railroad class for the CMSTP&P C-Liners was 16FF. The cabs weighed about 257,000 lbs. and the boosters 253,000 lbs.; length was about 57 feet.

The Springfield Line – New Haven C-Liners

The passenger C-Liners offered by FM included the CPA-24-5, a 2400 h.p. diesel with a 2-axle lead truck and a 3-axle truck in the rear. New Haven owned ten of the 22 units of this type built (790-799). The passenger C-Liner demonstrators 4801-4802 became New Haven 790-791 in 1951. 792-799 came to the NH in 1952. In addition to the New Haven locomotives, the other CPA-24-5 units were New York Central 4500-4507 and Long Island 2401-2404. One of the regular runs for the FM's was the line from New Haven, Connecticut, to Springfield, Massachusetts.

Below . . . 795 hustles south through Thompsonville, Connecticut, in 1954. *Upper Right* . . . Ex-demonstrator 4802, now New Haven 791 in railroad class DER-4 waits for departure time in Springfield, Mass. *Lower Right* . . . Five cars of New York bound passengers follow 794 out of Springfield in 1955.

Upper Left . . . FM 797 and an Alco DL109 sweep through a March snow with the 12:05 PM departure from Springfield. *Lower Left* . . . The *Day White Mountains*, Train 66, is north of Longmeadow, Massachusetts, behind the 791, that ex-FM demonstrator again. *Above* . . . C-Liners 790 and 797 are ready to move Train 53 out of Springfield in July 1954. The New Haven's 307,500 pound FM's were sold for scrap in 1962, a quite short service life of ten years from their 1950-1952 birth. 790 was Fairbanks-Morse demonstrator 4801 during 1950.

Above . . . The experimental lightweight low-slung Talgo train is on display in Springfield, Massachusetts, in July 1954. Almost towering over it on the adjacent track, NH 798 has just arrived from New Haven with a train from New York. *Right* . . . Train 77 departs Springfield behind the 791 in 1954 and the 794 in 1955. The FM's were painted hunters green with yellow striping during these years.

Westbound New York Central freight with a set of Alco FA's led by 1003 burbles past New Haven FM 794 in the Springfield, Massachusetts station at noon on October 15, 1954. Hundreds of EMD passenger E-units, and many Alco's too, were already in service when Fairbanks-Morse brought forth its C-Line. The passenger market for new diesels just was no longer that large, and FM sales never really had a chance to get rolling.

The Junior Train Master - H16-66

Beginning in 1951, Fairbanks-Morse put on the market an elongated version of their 4 wheel truck diesel road-switcher, the 1600 h.p. six wheel truck H16-66. The first locomotives of this type rode on cast truck frames and had the early design features created by Raymond Loewy for Fairbanks-Morse. Starting in 1954 the H16-66's were constructed in the same mold as the famous and slightly larger Train Master which first came out in 1953. With boxier lines and riding on tri-mount trucks, this newer version of the H16-66 became known as the Junior Train Master. Chicago & North Western 1699 shows the Junior Train Master lines at North Fond du Lac, Wisconsin.

Roster of H16-66 Locomotives (built 1951-1958)...
    Older style design ... 25 units
    C&NW 150, 1510-1514, 1605-1612, 168-172, 1668-1673
    Junior Train Master style ... 34 units
    C&NW 1674-1683, 1691-1700, 1901-1906 ... 26 units
    CMSTP&P 2125-2130   6 units
    SQUAW CREEK COAL CO. 721001   1 unit
    TENNESSEE VALLEY AUTHORITY 24   1 unit
Total of all H16-66 units ... 59
Note: MILW 2125-2130 renumbered to 550-555; 553-555 then renumbered to
    547-549; 547-552 then renumbered to 524-529.

Over the years the Chicago & North Western's fleet of H16-66 FM's spent much of their time in northern Wisconsin and Upper Michigan. By 1973 the remaining C&NW units worked mostly out of Green Bay, Escanaba, and the iron country of Upper Michigan. Among those remaining were the 1682 and the 1906. 1906 was the last H16-66 for the C&NW and was delivered in 1956. *Below* and *Upper Right* ... At the North Fond du Lac, Wisconsin yard, 1906 stands by the old roundhouse on a hot summer day, awaiting a call for a freight run northward in 1973. *Lower Right* ... In March 1974, 1682 was switching the yard on a sunny cool afternoon.

Of the thirty-four FM H16-66's in the Junior Train Master style, the C&NW had by far the most, twenty-six. Weights for the "Juniors" were mostly between 300,000 and 320,000 lbs., and the units were about 62 feet long. In recent years the outward appearance of the C&NW FM's has deteriorated; but inside, the tough, durable nature of the later FM designs persists. C&NW 1682 *(Above)*, 1699 *(Left)*, and 1906 *(Right)* pose in North Fond du Lac.

Upper Left . . . North Western H16-66 1682 drums across a small creek north of North Fond du Lac, Wisconsin. *Lower Left* . . . Milwaukee's six Junior Train Masters came as 2125-2130 but have been renumbered several times and are now 524-529. In 1972-1973 the 549 (now 526) and the 552 (now 529) were working in the St. Paul, Minnesota area. *Above* . . . 552 couples to a pair of cabooses as ex-CGW F-units of the C&NW chant past near Daytons Bluff in St. Paul. *Below* . . . C&NW 1699 moves out of the North Fond du Lac yard in August 1973.

GE - THE OLDEST AND THE NEWEST

General Electric is generally regarded as the producer of the first diesel-electric locomotives. The firm was the instigator of the project and carried out the locomotive assembly; however, the engines came from Ingersoll-Rand. The corporate existence of GE dates back to the 1890's; and by the early 1900's the firm produced motors and controls for street railway cars. General Electric then became engaged in the construction of electric mainline locomotives and gasoline powered rail cars for branch line service. The first of four gas-electric locomotives for the Minneapolis, St. Paul, Rochester & Dubuque Electric Traction Company were delivered in 1913. During the 1917-1918 period, GE turned out three diesel-electric locomotives which went to the Jay Street Connecting Railroad, the city of Baltimore, and the United States Army. Although plagued with problems, these units are generally considered the first diesel-electric locomotives.

Operational problems were resolved by 1923, and another unit was built. This locomotive was demonstrated during 1924 and eventually led to a General Electric/Ingersoll-Rand/American Locomotive Company engine built for the Central of New Jersey. CNJ No. 1000 went into service late in 1925, and was later billed as the "first commercially successful diesel-electric locomotive."

Between 1924 and 1928 GE continued working with Ingersoll-Rand and Alco, constructing a small number of diesel switchers. Assembly work was completed at GE's Erie, Pennsylvania, plant. During the 1930's and 1940's, GE produced and sold many small industrial switching locomotives, but it was in 1934 that executives decided not to undertake the building of full size railroad locomotives. The firm did, however, produce most of the electrical equipment used in mainline motive power constructed by other builders. It was

during this same year that Electro-Motive placed its diesel-power plant in Burlington's new *Zephyr* streamliner.

General Electric joined Alco in a marketing partnership beginning in 1940. This arrangement was not terminated until 1953 when GE began developing their own line of diesel locomotives. A 6000 h.p. four-unit set was tested extensively during the late 1950's all over the United States in various kinds of service. This testing culminated in the first two U25B's in 1959. This pair of units, Nos. 751-752, were tested on the Erie Railroad for some months and then demonstrated around the country during the early 1960's. Four more demonstrators were constructed in early 1961, Nos. 753-756. These newer U25B's incorporated some practical refinements desired by the railroads. The Union Pacific was the first to place an order for four U25 units, their numbers 625-628. The Frisco ordered eight units, four of which were new locomotives (Frisco 800-803) and four of which were the demonstrators Nos. 753-756 (Frisco Nos. 804-807).

Locomotive sales began to pick up in 1962. The U25 locomotives were designed for simplicity and ease of maintenance, just what the railroads were looking for in the days of increasing labor costs. Through the remaining years of the 1960's, GE gradually assumed the number two spot in diesel locomotive sales, overtaking Alco. General Electric's current line of locomotives is a gradual upgrading and refining of the original 2500 h.p. (U25), up to 3600 h.p. (U36) in 1973. With Alco's departure from the market in 1969, General Electric is now the only United States company competing with General Motors' Electro-Motive Division in the construction of new diesel-electric locomotives.

138

Union Pacific's U50

Above . . . Union Pacific U50 number 45 dwarfs trailing 3600 h.p. SD45's as they round the curve at Dale, Wyoming, westbound. Dale is where the newer line over Sherman Hill rejoins the older line (foreground). *Below* . . . 45 rolls along the Kaw River west of Kansas City, Kansas.

Two 2500 h.p. U25B's in one carbody, a 70 mph maximum speed, weight 556,000 lbs. loaded with fuel, and 83½ feet long, that's the General Electric U50 designed for the Union Pacific. *Upper Left* . . . U50 40 races west near Perry, Kansas, in 1970. *Lower Left* . . . Union Pacific's first U50, the 31, delivered in 1963, roars past the sign proclaiming Newman, Kansas, in 1971. *Below* . . . 39 is drifting to a stop in Muncie, Kansas, where the U50 will set out a couple of cars. It is late on a September afternoon and golden light reflects from the setting sun.

31 heads a westward freight departing Lawrence, Kansas, after picking up eight cars of locally originated traffic in March 1972. Overwhelming is the word for describing the size of the 5000 h.p. GE. Standing over sixteen feet tall, with virtually no short hood to break the effect of height, the U50 is imposing from all angles.

Above ... 31 rounds the curve past the station in Lawrence, Kansas, on its journey to North Platte, Nebraska. *Upper Right* ... 48 charges across a short bridge between Lawrence and Midland, Kansas. *Lower Right* ... 52 moves slowly through the Kansas City, Kansas, freight yard with an inbound in 1972.

Twenty-six of the dual-engined U50's were built by General Electric from mid-1963 to mid-1965. Union Pacific purchased 23 of them (numbered 31 to 53) and the other three went to the Southern Pacific. UP crews referred to the big GE's as "whirlybirds." One U50 was all the power needed for some freights, and sometimes an additional smaller diesel was added; when three or four U50's appeared together it was more rare. Here we have the range as one unit, the 44, gets an eastbound underway in Lawrence, Kansas, *Above*; and 52-31-51 thunder west near Topeka, Kansas in 1971, *Lower Right. Upper Right* . . . For some months in 1970, UP 31 ran with the access door panels removed. Here the engineer is waiting for the blue inspection flag to be removed in Kansas City, Kansas in June 1970. The double-engine concept can easily be seen with two of almost everything visible inside. The Kansas City-North Platte, Nebraska, run was one of the main haunts of the U50's. In the fall of 1969, Union Pacific started receiving forty more similar locomotives, the U50C, numbers 5000-5039. They ride on six wheel trucks rather than the two sets of four wheel trucks under each end of the older U50's.

146

On April 12, 1971, Union Pacific 41 was running east in the company of two Southern Pacific SD's. *Above* . . . Near Muncie, Kansas. *Below* . . . Roaring past the Bonner Springs, Kansas station. In late 1973 the UP began trading in some of the U50's on new U30C locomotives.

In September 1970, GE's 40 and 36 are about ready to depart Kansas City. *Following Page* . . . 40 rolls through the small Kansas settlement of Williamstown; and U50 44 races west under a low December sun east of Perry, Kansas in 1968.

U28C

As was indicated in the introduction to the General Electric section, GE's single-engine designs have been essentially a gradual upgrading and refining of the original 2500 h.p. U25 design. The four wheel truck U25B was supplemented in 1963 by a six wheel truck unit on a somewhat longer frame, the U25C. At the end of 1965 power output was increased to 2800 h.p. thus creating the U28B and U28C. A further increase to 3000 h.p. in late 1966 brought about the U30 line. The U28C locomotives covered in this section were therefore one step in this evolution, essentially covering the calendar year 1966. *Above* . . . Nearly new Burlington U28C's 566-573-574 are emerging from the west end of Clyde Yard in early April 1966.

Above . . . CB&Q 566-573-574 in Clyde Yard-Cicero, Illinois. *Below* . . . BN U28C 5664 (ex-CB&Q 576) and GP20 2029 are methodically rolling a train of empty coal hoppers westward between Hinckley, Illinois and Mored siding in 1973.

Below . . . In the fall of 1969, Q 566 and Erie-Lackawanna 3633-3634 are pooled on Train 97 at Shabbona, Illinois. Exterior design of the U28C changed slightly during the year they were constructed (compare CB&Q/BN units with UP).

Above ... BN 5674 (ex-Northern Pacific 2808) rolls ponderously over the Rock Island main in Joliet, Illinois, with a coal train. This BN train of Montana coal is routed the last few miles from Chicago to the outskirts of Joliet on the Illinois Central Gulf. *Below* ... The newer U30C 5359 of the Burlington Northern eases by U28C 5664 and GP20 2029 at West Eola, Illinois, in 1973. The 5664 still wears its red, white, and grey CB&Q colors.

GE built 71 of the U28C locomotives, plus ten U28CG units for passenger service on the Santa Fe. Union Pacific employs ten of the 67 foot long units, 2800-2809. *Above* . . . 2804 heads a mix of EMD and GE units west through Lawrence, Kansas, in April 1970. *Right* . . . 2800, 2801, an earlier U25B, and an EMD unit are moving east through a spring dust storm near Topeka, Kansas. *Far Right*, . . . Penn Central 6534 (ex-PRR 6534 and still lettered for the Pennsy) is easing past the platform at Englewood Station in Chicago with an overnight train from the east in April 1969. *Lower Far Right* . . . UP 2801 and 2809 at Lawrence.

In 1966 the AT&SF put into service ten U28CG (for steam generator) locomotives numbered 350-359. Initial use of these diesels was on the *Texas Chief*, Trains 15 and 16. Because steam generator space had been provided in the original design, the 350 class was no longer than the regular U28C. The group was renumbered to 7900-7909 during the 1969-1970 renumbering and shifted into freight service. Generally they work in the Corwith-Argentine pool with some service to Texas. *Above ...* 7901 hammers the diamond in Joliet on the point of *Super C* westbound in August 1970. *Left ...* 359 is only moments away from the bumper post in Dearborn Station, Chicago, with the *Texas Chief.*

Above . . . The three GE's off Train 16 have been separated and the 352 is about to ease off the turntable into a stall in Chicago's 18th Street diesel facility for servicing in October 1966. Roster of U28C's: UP 2800-2809, SP 7150-7159, PC (ex-PRR) 6520-6534, BN 5650-5665 (ex-CB&Q 562-577), BN 5666-5677 (ex-NP 2800-2811), L&N 1526-1533 (1533 was renumbered from 1525). Total: 71 units. Note: PRR 6516-6519 were built December 1965 in U25C body with U28C horsepower. As has been mentioned the GE line was a continual process of evolution making for some overlapping of locomotive types.

Above . . . Union Pacific's Alco switcher 1112 is about to swing away from the main to proceed up the Leavenworth branch as U28C 2804 heads west on the outskirts of Lawrence, Kansas. *Below* . . . UP 2804, GP30B 706, and a real rarity, Alco C855 60 roar eastward near Hershey, Nebraska. A late afternoon sun gleams off the consist in May 1968.

A much weaker December sunset reflects off a Union Pacific U28C-EMD SD24B combination westbound at Linwood, Kansas. GE and EMD units . . . a fitting end to a look at the American diesel, for in 1975 they were the two remaining U. S. locomotive builders.

Timetable of Events
in the
Evolution of the Diesel-Electric Locomotive

1913 — General Electric builds first gas-electric locomotive

1918 — General Electric builds first diesel-electric locomotives

1922 — Electro-Motive Corporation established to sell gas-electric railcars

1924 — General Electric builds their first successful diesel-electric

1925 — Central of New Jersey 1000 in service

— Baldwin Locomotive Works builds their first experimental diesel-electric

1928 — American Locomotive Company builds 3 experimental diesels for New York Central

1930 — General Motors purchases Electro-Motive Corporation and Winton

1931 — American Locomotive Company's first self-generated diesel venture

1932 — Fairbanks-Morse opposed-piston engine for U.S. Navy

1934 — Chicago, Burlington & Quincy and Union Pacific streamliners with Winton engines

— General Electric decides not to make large diesel units of its own

1935 — Electro-Motive Corporation's first box-cab road diesels

— EMC's first switchers

— EMC starts new plant near La Grange, Illinois

— American Locomotive Company engines used to power Gulf, Mobile & Northern *Rebels*

1936 — Baldwin Locomotive Works first switcher with De La Vergne engine

1937 — Electro-Motive Corporation builds EA's for Baltimore & Ohio, E1's for Santa Fe, and E2's for Union Pacific

1938 — EMC adopts new engine, own traction equipment

1939 — EMC builds first FT freight diesel demonstrator and passenger E3's

— Baldwin Locomotive Works offering line of switchers

— Fairbanks-Morse opposed-piston engine in Southern Railway railcars

1940 — American Locomotive Company builds their first passenger diesel, the DL109

— Alco-General Electric marketing established

1941 — First revenue run of FT from Electro-Motive Corporation on Santa Fe

— Electro-Motive Corporation/Winton Engine merged into General Motors

— Alco builds first road-switcher type diesel

1944 — Fairbanks-Morse builds its first diesels

— Alco builds last of 4-8-8-4 *Big Boy* steam locomotives for the Union Pacific

1945 — Baldwin Locomotive Works builds its first road units

1946 — Alco builds first PA's

1948 — Electro-Motive Division builds their first road-switcher (BL)

— General Electric builds experimental gas turbine locomotive

— Alco builds its last steam locomotive

1949 — Electro-Motive Division builds first GP7

— Baldwin builds their last steam locomotive

— Lima Locomotive Works builds its last steam locomotive

— First U.S. major railroad dieselized

— Baldwin puts sharknose design on diesels

1953 — Fairbanks-Morse builds the *Train Master*

— General Electric leaves Alco-GE marketing partnership

1956 — Baldwin builds its last diesel locomotive

— Alco Products becomes name for American Locomotive Company

1958 — Fairbanks-Morse builds their last diesel for U.S. railroads

1959 — General Electric builds first U25 demonstrators

1960 — General Electric announces entry into diesel market with U25

1962 — General Electric sales start to pick up

1963 — Alco *Century* series locomotives announced

— Fairbanks-Morse builds last diesel (for Mexico)

— General Electric builds U50 (dual-engined diesel)

— Electro-Motive builds DD35B (dual-engined diesel)

1969 — Alco builds its last diesel

— Electro-Motive builds largest diesel (dual-engined DDA40X for Union Pacific)

1972 — Electro-Motive Division's 50th anniversary

1974 — 50th anniversary of General Electric's first successful diesel-electric

160